W0006314

RINGS

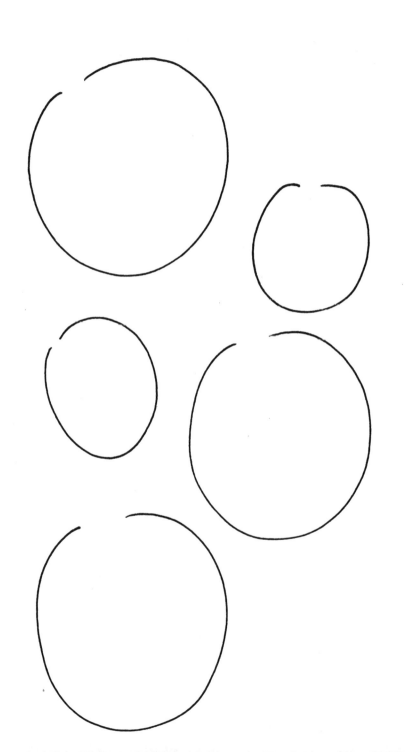

Rings

JASMINE DREAME WAGNER

KELSEY STREET PRESS

FIRSTS!

KELSEY STREET PRESS

2824 Kelsey Street, Berkeley, CA 94705

info@kelseyst.com www.kelseyst.com

Library of Congress Cataloging-in-Publication Data

Wagner, Jasmine Dreame.

[Poems. Selections]

Rings / Jasmine Dreame Wagner.

pages cm. — (Firsts!)

ISBN 978-0-932716-83-5 (pbk. : acid-free paper)

I. Title.

PS3623.A356304A6 2014

811'.6—dc23

2014023620

Designed by Quemadura

Illustration on cover and p. ii by Jasmine Dreame Wagner

Typefaces designed by Sibylle Hagmann and Zuzana Licko

Edited by Anna Soteria Morrison and Valerie Witte

Printed on acid-free, recycled paper

in the United States of America

FOR MY MOTHER

Contents

''LIKE EMPIRES AND LANGUAGES''

3

''AFTER THE AIR FORCE—EVACUATE EXPOSED''

7

''EVENTUALLY, EVERYONE''

14

''GREENPOINT TERMINAL MARKET''

15

''FAVOR IS AN ARBITRARY SEED—INTO ITS AIRSHAFT''

29

''IT TURNS OUT, IT WAS ADVERTISING''

38

''V. I. LENIN PALACE OF CULTURE AND SPORT''

40

''KEY OF C—YOU PRESERVE WHAT QUICKENS''

49

''QUESTION MY MOTIVES, ASK ME MY NAME''

57

''RIDERDUST (THE FAIRGROUNDS)''

58

''SO REMEMBER—THE STALKS OF SUMAC''

75

''MY SISTER, MY SECRETARY''

81

''CHAMPION MILL''

83

''DO YOU TURN ON YOUR TELEVISION—ZIRCONIUM RODS''

93

''ADZE, BECAUSE''

98

''AMERICAN FLAGS''

100

''THE DEAD C SCROLLS''

111

NOTES

115

ACKNOWLEDGMENTS

116

RINGS

LIKE EMPIRES AND LANGUAGES

Marilyn wore
many rings,

and a redwood's worth
of layered skirts.

When she stood at the center
of Times Square

and confessed
our questions,

a light changed
from green to red

like birdsong,
interrupted.

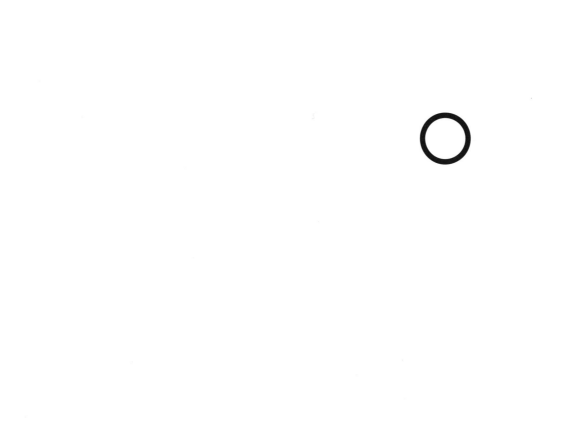

After the air force.

After the construction paper tulips.
After the icicles slip.

After the election,
after the left hand feigns cursive,
a garage door closes. A sparrow attacks an almond.

A static of gnats spackles a window as
a stucco ceiling, a yellow balloon—
An ageless agave spiking as
a minute molds an onion beneath a refrigerator bulb. As

an amber bracelet brandishes a scorpion thorax,
an article discarded, yesterday's burnt match. As yesterday itself is
an artifact, an amaryllis laid against

an arsonist's white fencepost. As
an arsonist warns his long-lost brother about
a cobra in a basket in a dream he had of hunting

as dust motes
as echoes echo

as feathered leaves pardon a flock

as graffiti and gnarled roots grip a grate

as houses huddle around their cul-de-sac

as it becomes obvious that life is lived in spite of consequence

as tomorrow, an aleatory composition,

a lichen, its growth will augur decay.

As an envelope laced with an opaque powder is

a puddle imprinting on rain, as rains imprint on rice paddies,

a satellite dish, the cold-wash laundry, the thrashed pink disposables.

As a television whittles its folk silent

as a saw by an antler chucked in a bush, or

a terminator seed under an aluminum heat lamp

a termite nest after a pesticide treatment

a thumbnail sketch of an assassin.

A town pool at midnight.

Autofocus

Baby, baby you know you—

Baby, fix me and just shake me—

Baby, baby, it's a wild world—

Baby, one more time—

Back at the farmhouse,
        ball lightning bends the broadcast.
Bats skate across the tension
        beyond the bay window, where

      a bayou moon decanting sorrow from soil
    blooms like a bestseller over the basin. Because

a city aspires to the starkness of glass. Because
we have no fortune like a copse of wild thyme. Because
brothers ante-up in a game of blackjack. Because
beauty, like a bouquet, is embossed in brass
      because beauty aspires to body
      and body aspires to build and break
      and buildings breach

            because hunger is a property of mass. Because scabs
        bleed when brushed, a beacon whorls its flare onto the beach.
      Because only a concept escapes unscathed

  before painting lead pipes with lead paint
between bank vault seams in the walls of the pressurized cabin. Because
before story, there was sequence—a branch
      between hawks' silhouettes, where now, we see
      black knots of pine cross, like a suture, the crevasse.

     Black silos bloom inside our bodies.

By the hand, take me by the hand, pretty mama—
By the hand—

      Can't quit you, baby—
          Carpenter, your simple love uses all varieties of wrench.
          Cakes spin in their cases. Clouds seed
chalky violet candy CHECKS CASHED
          Come and dance with your daddy—
                    "Come home" *all night long.* / Bangle and bangle-
          charm, chime and collusion, our crippled cache

             catalogue of the digital core of the
                    comfort of objects ("—those cherry blossoms
                      can't be real! Can they?")

                              Cloud seeds. The sky's cracked
                          corridors. Jets scrape
                          condensation from the runnels as

                              commercials
                compete for mirrors at the county fair.

      Consider who is standing outside
     their continuity, as what is
       cosmetic rises to its surface:

The cherry blossoms aren't real.
The crabapples aren't real either,
and crabgrass has everything to do with perpetual longing
as our country of just outrageous desserts
a circus tent collapses from

cut corner to / cut corner

through a cosmology of corn
through countdown procedures
through court cases and codes
through planned communities and chat rooms

could you kiss me on the cheek without confronting the artifice?

Count the black sedans in the courtyard.
Count the cruise ships placidly leaning.
Count the dammed leaves choking the drain.
Count the elegant neckties on the revolving velveteen rack.
Count February's crows scribbling in snow as
deer in the yard make a framing gesture,
describe their year using only bankrupt antlers.

December, February, months come and go as
Debussy dreams of a piano without hammers
deep in the calendar's centerfold

where dawn breaks over latched gates, vanity plates, frost dust
draped over the mosque's epaulets, the temple's lapels, the churches' cigarettes,
the daycare center's Dobermans dreaming maybe of ducks and drakes
as daylight darns the world's rough hedges with silver-
dollar filaments of storm drains and tracery thin as shades
of degree between frozen and freezing

or shades of degree between belief and believing.
Dumb it down, the brother says, deal the cards, but he knows he
doesn't mean what he's saying. At the farmhouse, the TV's
dialed in to the races. An eye on the track, his brother
draws the diamond jack, says, brother, how
did I

dig a hole? Did I

dismantle a dove's broken ribs purely

to divest its wishbone
                                              divining rod, coat of feathers?
Your distressed denim is dissolving,
                                              your unemployed debutante daughter,
her dithering gold lamé epigraph,
                                              antidepressants. Don't discount her dread
as endemic of extended adolescence.
                                              Some boldface afternoons, all she sees are
dolphins and disciples of
                                              Unitarian congregations. Don't drag her

into your inchoate department

                              where disheveled stars smoke cigars in the dusk's

due diligence

                       where deer ticks draw and expel the new moon. Traffic

drones

               where there are no roads. In the klieg lights, goldfinches flicker

like DOE

                   sprockets. Draw a vial of oil to determine the payload, but

don't spell

                 for her your thrill of ripping limbs from crickets.

   Don't tell her

                   she's delicate unless you want her to break.

      Doors locked

                 by magnets fly open into September's

      dusty marigolds,

                  shapes older than maps, where

              each fleck of paint is a thin pain, where

                every day's a dollar

                 every day counts

electric neon cowgirls flash their thighs sixty times a minute where
we

                            Evacuate

                            Exposed

(Eventually, everyone
in the future will have
15 minutes of energy
Eventually, everyone
in the future will have
15 minutes of privacy
Eventually, everyone

will sleep automatically,
will come full-circle, will
evolve to see they've
ended where they started
Where everyone will
evolve to see in frames
everyone eventually

will be the primary
caregiver, the primary
caretaker, the only one
in charge of everything
Eventually, everyone will
be a branch manager
of the consolidated dream

GREENPOINT TERMINAL MARKET

Follow the yellow line to
      the yellow weeds in their
            yellow ditches: gasoline,
one rosebud match to spark and
      burn like a television.

Paranormal glow of the
    Citicorp Center, aqua-
        marine of a caged parrot.

Ruin is a cultured pearl.

Rain comes as requirement.

    Requires we submit to
its loose, fluted memory
    fluttering like a receipt

        in the incision, human-
colored haze in the hollow
    sector. Iron sleeves of drain-
        age where pigeons in wire-
less slate skies return to roost,

        lucite-winged moths narrowing
            beneath sodium streetlamps

                dim

        as the maples in the park
        turn
                on—

Sleep without memory, our

ruin.

Past deferred from becoming
           passed, from emerging legend
in the foreground of trauma,

ruin itself, traumatic.

Its fingerbone begs us to
           unearth its contusions from

corridors of lightning-singed
           Christmas holly. Ruin is

                    forensic, identity
        as many forms of erasure

            as preservation: coin-toss
                        distribution of spiders,

            dandelions in bluegrass
                        where bulbs of black brands curl from
    milkweed sown in sow thistle:
                wax myrtle coils, smokestacks

                    titanium light has cursed
        with specificity, each
                    raw wire, each cinquefoil
    chrysanthemum equally
                        alight in terse, unrehearsed
        testimony that marks their
                place as *site*.

—from the northern
whirlpool of Spuyten Duyvil
to the southern breach of time-
lapsed barges' haul, the Narrows,
the East River under gold-
leaf, rippling, oil-steeped welt
coal-thick with potential, its
pillars of pyrite, jagged

skyline hazardous with zinc,
cadmium, thallium, lead,
benzene, silver, osmium,
nickel, carbon monoxide,
sulfuric acid, rubber,
asbestos, arsenic and
fiberglass—

    —from the open field to the
            curtilage, to the tag-pocked
hull, stripped with chemical wash,

     from desire to rumor

        from dynamite to fiber-
           optics, from arson coeval

       to vagrant, to armed guard, to
hex, to diode, to copper-
   barred bales of synthetic knits,
       polyester butterfly
collars, silk crêpe ruching, shirred
   crates of marjoram rot

     burnt—

In the end, a fly dies as
flies die.
        Our rust, not our fear,
configures the elements.

Ruin is a misspelled word.

Our ruin comes secondhand,
like clothes.
        Radium buried
in an ingrown nail.
          Footprints
like neologisms we
cannot reverse.
        Ruin is
a cask of flies.
        Neither dead
nor alive, the mass.
        In the
end, a fly dies as flies die.

        .

When a body moves within
ruin,
      the body becomes
the impasse within its core.

The ruin becomes a cask.

The body becomes a cask.

All that becomes,
              becomes a
cask.
      All that becomes,
              becomes
a core.
       Ruin is not meant
to be amplified,
         though it
is bought and sold as more,
             more.

When a body moves within
ruin,
      the body becomes
remains.
          Not meant to be named,
a body is not a name

for a body is not meant

to be covered.
          Ruin is
not memory,
          though it steeps
its ward *in memoriam*

more often than not.
          Ruin
is *naught* and *knot* and *ø,*
            as
ruin *should* and *could* and *ought*

and when, in the scabbard of

kite and *cot* and *caught*,

is wrought.

Dust filming the lung of a hepafilter. Clotting the blades of a white

plastic desk fan. Red lettuce leaf, heirloom tomato. Cloud oil, cider

vinegar. Satellite in a stone statuary. Drywall between iron pylons

accreted along McCarren Park. Meridians of cathedrals cached

under glass atria. Asterisks. Camels along the Dead Sea. Bauhaus.

Dried mackerel strung from coarse hemp twine. Green vireo born

with one bent wing. Cellular transport. Cubed styrofoam. Charcoal.

Favor is an arbitrary seed.

                              (Names of
                          flowers: true or
                                       false?
            Feral hackgrass. Bitchweed. Black-Eyed Susans.
            Fecalvine. Chafeblossom. Rapeseed and phlox.)
                  Some flowers make us feel like our
fingernail's been scraped by a paperclip
and some flowers make us *feel*

and the fact is: we
fall for the names of flowers the way we
fall for the names of chains of superspeedways: Daytona, Pocono, Talladega . . .
and the fact is: we snip at the base of a potted plant and pluck
a flower from its ring
and the fact is: though our intentions are good, we warm a plate in the microwave
and forget the fork
        as flashes of aluminum filaments
flare along the fire-resistant lining. This isn't about
        flight emulation or parasympathetic physical reaction, this isn't about
fistfights or factory farms, it isn't
        fasting for social change or feasting in celebration of it. The fact is, fear

is the foundation of what we find here, where we
fast-forward to the tire blowout, where we,
from our frosting to our fat-free filling,
from the fins of sharks preserved in formaldehyde
to the fragments of feeling that race from feed to feed,
from a distance are evergreens repeatable as memes. Remember?

For centuries, war was a rumor. There was
fortune, but there wasn't fame. In fact, there wasn't much
to fear until the dust clouds fomented. Few could see the trees
for the fringe, the forest for its foreign language. It's true,
form eventually followed function. But how could we
forget the unformulated ripening of the pear, the thrill of play, the fractal pip of
our fingertip? From the red-lipped rose
flush with alliteration to the maximalism (and lack) of what is
found there, ambiguous loss is unfinished business.
And as a fad that fell from fashion
rebounds for a final round, we cut and rearrange our blooms
to forge the feeling we once found
in familiarity: forsythia forked; the twins down the street, pickled into men;
the false-bottom box of finality. Now, if only our austerity
fetish could afford to lend us a frame
from the film we're sure will surface
after we've finished

our glossary of gem-studded growing pains:

one garlic clove (virtual, for the glittering CGI vampires)

two grommets, two deadbolts (to keep the fray at bay)

three glossy magazines (stilettos, a streetlight's tangerine
        glaze,
a geranium's girth, its red pom-poms, cheerleader glee)

four girls (fierce and gaudy as blown glass) who are
grown versions of gabby dolls and western gunplay

                ("My god, how many years define a
        generation now, anyways?")

five gradated drawings of cave paintings, proof of
grief, primitive, burned to glyph, now a
grade school science project

six grams of gold
seven guineafowl
                a globe, an apple, a pen

a God who butters his bread on both sides of the bread

        where grifters, guildsmen, gilded children
    ground the wires, adjust the gain
in the GIANT GARDEN STADIUM
where the GREATEST ENTERTAINER ALIVE
        guides us through

the gradual deconstruction of gaze

the gradual desaturation of image

the gradual depigmentation of skin

the gradual denaturation of uranium

the gradual unhinging of hips

the gradual unschooling of prejudice

the gradual unspooling of thread

the gradual untooling of anything "good" (so the critics claim)

blogging from the greenhouse where our

girls are seeded, sheltered, sunned, tanned, trimmed, tuned, and watered until they're

good and ready, from their vocal fry and

glottal stops to their abject

giddiness as though they've been gagged and laughing-

gassed. A girl is a military clearance. A girl is a brass vase. A girl is a cave of violets. A girl is our

greatest living entertainer and her girlfriends are the

genius gatekeepers born to demigods who once were

girls. Their intricate

grillwork keeps us going through aggregated global indices of

Gambling losses, the;

Gas gauges, the; (see *Gasoline*);

Gasoline, (see *Gods*);

Geiger counter, (clicks of); (debris, of tsunami);

Gifts, (for seven holidays); (including the calendar needed to repeat them);

Gods, (loneliness independent of belief in); (sacrifice in name of);

Gouge, (knife-); (price-, see *Gasoline*);

Gowns, (bridal); (Crillon Ball); (designer); (discount); (evening); (luxury); (monster); (Oscars, see *Gods*); (prom); (sequin); (slutty); (strapless); (Supreme Court, see *Gods*); (red carpet, see *Gods*); (vintage); (wedding); (wholesalers of); **Guns**, (accessories, see *Gifts*); (airport restrictions); (belonging to father, see *Gods*); (bullets, silver, see *Gifts*); (concealment of); (funeral salute); (Glock pistol); (holding, how it feels, see *Gods*); (NRA stance on ownership); (paintball, see *Gifts*); (porcelain); (pointed, see *Gods*); (trading of, see *Gifts*); (vintage); (wholesalers of);

as halfway through the hour, the game show
host hesitates, then hints: *"Have you ever bet on horses?"*

His audience has never heard anything so
hilarious and in the heat of the moment, the joke is hot and off-hue as

his hair, rouged with henna. His headlights myopic in the mist as

he hops home from happy hour through the
    hot black mulch of chicory, the
            horizon striped like a Navajo blanket, its
    hallucination marmalade-thick in the
hazy hierarchy of airborne particles and scattered light.

Harmonies of air conditioners hum along his hallway.
How did he arrive, at this moment, so close to the sun? And
    how far beneath his surface must we dig? To find

            hope in the harness as the
            racehorse hugs the inside track.

[33]

However we lost our taste for commandments,
hurricane names switchback through the warren.

Humidity holds its breath
and hiccups, disrupts
the heat wave's continuity
that heralds a crack in the house of cards,
the haunted seasons (clouds are a haunted house as a word is a haunted house)
the halo of horror in the hot ash that stripes the
hillsides in a chocolate fudge ripple (the abnormal karyotype, the jet stream, the isotope,
the highway, the guilty grooming it).

How long will the car run on empty?
How do we know if the medicine is working?
How do we know if our message has been read? How do we know
how many paces from here until the end of the century? How and where
did you hone your skill for blowing smoke rings? Is it the way
you bite your tongue, hold your lower lip, hide your cigarette? Who taught you
how to filter and inhale/exhale a collective breath? Politics/a cigar doesn't end
stubbed out in a dish, or in handcuffs, a spattering of
handclaps. There is no *ends*. History doesn't sprint to a finish.
Histrionic as we are, we are
host and hostess to an evolving alphabet. We are witness

to our voice in the playback. When the whistle blows.
When it's our *out*, our red card, our shame, our bench, our unemployment.
Our hangover. We are the ruler that harbors no hash marks. We are

the heroes our culture requires, gold stars
on our hands and on our foreheads and we
      can always add one more
          to our daisy chain
          to our crescent of blemishes
          to our broadband seismic waveform
          to our adolescent rite, repeated and repeatable
     as the hierarchies of pop
harmonies and fraternity hazing. We'll huddle and screw. We'll play

house because we can't play
homeowner. We'll play

     and hear whatever sound is promoted through the
          hound dog yowling, the haunted graffiti in the
     histamine of hyphy
held up on the overpass in high volume traffic, we can
hear it when we press our ears against our Hi-Def sets. We can
feel it when we press our palms against a loved one's chest. We can
hear the phasing signal comping every passing wave, yes, we can
hear it, okay? Have you heard? We can. Hear it any way we'd like, for free
and I admit

I can't remember anyone's name.
I can't remember anyone's number.
I choose to notice the singular
          icicle,

the identical briefcases at the pay phone in the airport.
I know that every time I see something, I should say something
but I don't want to consider cruelty or what we neglect to save,
          the idle engines on moonlit cliffs, the last still at the drive-in.

I feign hunger in order to exploit your propensity to give.
I hoard a grain of sand.
I listen as my grain rattles in the depths of a paper bag.
I improvise
          an ashtray, a Persian rug, a world racked with cruelty

               In bark, unending asperity
               In mines of indeterminate substance, I see   how

impossible it is to remove the crowbar from the memory of the crow, how
impossible it is to remove the crowbar from the memory of the crowbar, how
          in sheath-like pods of catalpa trees, sphinx moths feed
               in the translucence above the arboretum's filaments
               in the length of time it takes sweat to bead
               in the dirigible of day

               into the fog where it is thin and waif-like—
               Irises pressed in flint.

                                                  Is it raining, or
                                                  is the city rising into steam?

                                        I stare directly

                        into the cloud,

                into oncoming traffic,
        into the irrepressible meaning

            inherent in our digital history
                                        I stare directly

                    into the stream . . .
            into the black spade beyond narrative . . .

                        It's a star-eat-star universe out there

                        and its sound
                is only a song, but all that
                is real contains a specter of
                    its airshaft—

(It turns out, it was advertising. There was no higher calling.

It turns out, some things speak truth inaccurately, like a light wash over a jpeg of my dinner on Instagram.

It turns out, my childhood friend once challenged me to a game.

In the game, we ran along the beach, scrawling words in the sand.

It turns out, most words intact by sunset wins.

It turns out, she knew the tide line better than I did.

It turns out, her last remaining word was "Justice."

It turns out, a gull's tracks can run like serifs across the sand.

It turns out, like most handwritten drafts, they are unreadable but necessary.

It turns out, our youth was digitally reformatted to stream at a faster frame rate.

It turns out, my friend is a banker now. Vice President of First Federal Bank of Boston.

It turns out,

I'm a poet.

It turns out, the use of anaphora and spondee in "Five / Five dollar / Five dollar footlong" is immensely satisfying.

It turns out, the commercials are written during the commercial breaks.

V. I. LENIN PALACE OF CULTURE AND SPORT

Place your mouth on my palm—

LEAD a thoroughbred on a leash, quilt a topological map, then—grouse, knuckle, delta. No incorporation, just: wrought bodies, heifer's maws, tousled branches, then—*but a surface lives, it has been born.* How what is known shapes what is not known, hued by a palette of command: plate glass constrained by its own internal friction. Its vice versa, the broken dishes, unlimited edition. Beneath a concrete hull, a lone transistor winches an engine. Beneath wormholes, their electromagnetic impact. The viola's sour pink muzak. Do you know how sibilance grades, elongates absences? Do you know how neglect bleaches a flute of its process? As most words known aren't navigable roads. As most words used are heavy metals, migration.

Taste my pulse, call it honeysuckle—

WHAT MOVES and what does not move, in heavy metals, migration? What desire to dagger downward against movement against? Then seep into leech, into magnet. What is radioactive spirals outward. What is radioactive intends, as over, over again, contents resist their packaging. Ink blot. Milk spilt. Fireworks. A starling's yaw, a starboard zag, a getaway car. A vandal's black mirror well. A meteor, expired and expiring, in a coat pocket. Detected by a method by which our eyes are fruit no one can eat. By which our fruits are seagulls chained to a revolving door hunger, our deficit smelted to the moment's bloc. As, alone in the perfumery, the Rachmaninoff performs itself, a tomb-rubbing, a graft spelt. As, alone on the court, love of the same embraces the same. *Don't struggle. Come in. You're welcome.*

Yellow can be blue if we say it's so—

WHAT IS FRAGILE must break early. Some porcelain, recipes, classified documents. And lacquered mercury-chewed hat brims. And asbestos licks, tics of tide table indexes. As scribbles of lacquer and consonants remain. Some in a thumbprint as the whorl of days shirks requirements. Dandelions simper, offer themselves as their substitute sacrifice. Bald streetlights line up as though they were in a cop show. What proof: braille of rain on windows, pollen in a pool of piss? What cannot prove: hurled cloud, hinges of taxis and patience? Grain buckles a lens. Reverb suckles a bootstrap. One cannot lend audible depth to an ice cube until it begs, bleats water, and water cannot retrace its steps. Write the rule one hundred times on the dry erase board: one must count incrementally to thunder. But by the time time is understood, it is already too late.

For instance, the sky is a dandelion of church fire—

SO MUCH CEMENT, so many hedges, topiary, dips and blades to choose from. Canned feathers, candid camera, one is already behind a gate. Behind the plumage of paint chips, the remains of decommissioned holidays narrate *no entry*, as a broken plate can't narrate dinner. As airborne filigree can't orate an archipelago, even if every island is an ear, burning to rumor. What we learn from baseball can't translate here, where a float dazzles the flow of traffic the way an earmarked wing sizzles in a dish. We can bequest a wreck, but the gift is echo. Reflecting fractions of dividends/lemons. Even puddles genuflect in the primacy of representations. A box top on the stair where a holler was hijacked. A ribbon in a bow beside it.

In the stairwell, the echoing stairwell—

WHAT REMAINS after glass is a grave. As a shower drains, bile squeaks from a spleen, a stomach carries a grudge against silk. Bile hollows its troughs the way one uses a fork to pick cigarette butts from a blender. In the lottery of batteries, track marks and poppy seed confetti— In the lottery of hand-scored sports statistics, of words traded for branded names— In the lottery of being born again in the leaf pile— Of being the cause of our rejection of causes— Of gravity drinking our appendages into our withers, first as an act of magic, then ritual, then torture. Radio waves pierce us. We hear them coming. Is what remains, after they have passed, adolescence? Is what remains, after they have passed, *amber waves*? Who can remember what one wished on candles? What child's wish for sweets is manifested in a rage?

AND WHAT DRIVES
us to make love

or anything, really?
Dreams

of moneybags and goldbricks, era
of shipwrecks, your pirates swam to sand.
With what will

we tow ourselves?
Limericks? Marshmallows? Peonies?

Alone in the stadium, Love of the Game
and The Game

embrace.

—Drive. Where to?
Anywhere.

Key of C: No Black Keys.

       (Look. A key is a prime example of how
language imposes limits on what we can know,
                      OK?)

Let's let loose
Let's line up our
lawn chairs on the Hollywood Hills,
light up the switchboards, sing "Happy Birthday"

Let's illuminate everything we can
lay a finger on:
the lights you see when you close your eyes and press your fingers on the lids
the lights that snake down Broadway as you lean against the window in the backseat of a taxi
the last crepuscular spokes to crack the clouds above the prairie

as we listen through the veil of radio
to the limit of our nation-state defended at a frontier

as we loiter on the border of hearsay and hit-making
Let's light up

the lunules and ferrules, the little things we never knew had names
the leftover lines that linger, like

Your hand is a ground zero of tenderness.
Your instrument gains sentience as you play.
Your kite in a white sky, you've changed and have been changed.
Your lottery ticket has a natural history.
Your man stands where he's been told to stand.
Your neutral milk hotel is a secure green zone for cattle to graze
and an orange is the reason you are not a panther

and losing isn't permanent, you only
lose an object once before its space is pregnant
like an elaborate seasonal costume or the convoluted smell
of lavender, lemongrass, liver and lettuce. You shouldn't wear your
longing for all to witness. Save something for yourself. Listen to the crickets,
learn to untie a tie as you pause on the middle stair between the living room and oblivion.
Loss is important. It's the only thing that's certain. There's nothing
like it

    and we can't "like" it

    the way we like a grove of lilacs
    the way we like the way our gold tip pen scrawls our tag on a downtown bank
    the way we like to lick our lollipops until our tongues turn green
    like lights when we're lucky and not at all late, yellow
    like lemon juice on the shells along the jetty
    like the liver filters heavy metals
    like the ocean's mercury

        and mercury's memory
        and memory's cornfield

of manuals, mash-ups and merchandise
where Mars tips in its ellipsis
where a mannequin stands straight, turns, waves
as the melody modulates, where a pardoned
martyr hangs

multiple boughs of mistletoe that in turn resemble
moon cycle charts, bowls of steamed mussels,
mossy cataracts on cobblestones,
men in velvet vestments in monthly magazines

where men with flashlights cut like swordfish
through midnight in a frost-flecked minefield.

Where milk thistle rockets unclasp.
Where momentum accrues like debt along a county line.

Where multiple empires of beverages contend for a title.
Where most of what is written is written in rhyme.

Moths bore holes in its pink cardigan.
Need's unending knit. Where

there is no medicine to modify the meter
the moment the needle hits. Where

the monophonic record spins and spins. Where
our moon hangs like a neon clock
over its monopoly of meadows, we are

neither fingerprint wipe nor breadcrumb trail

neither nettles, their patient spooks, nor neutrinos, their impartiality

neither medieval neume nor Newtonian notation

not a gnarled guardrail

never a darkened auditorium

and normal is a cycle on a washing machine

where new bubbles rise and are rinsed, where new nouns are

nicked in picnic tables, pinned on pages, new signal paths, new nominal levels

enumerated and where the numbers fail us, we compose

a novel or a new mathematical language

to explain the noose at the center of the universe

as the natural world bristles in its fractal snow

as northern lights come down in its theater

as a necklace glitters on a velvet cube. Never mind

the nose ring. At one point in time, the null set,

the notion that we could build a nest for nothing with no safety

net was inconceivable. Now,

a foreclosed creek has two opposing banks. We have multiple.

No question anticipates a creek's capacity, its revenue inlet, its irreversible flow,

no algorithm predicts its buoyancy (or lack of it). Not a magnesium flashbulb,

not a smutty magazine, not a search engine optimized content factory.

News breaks like shoddy fakes of novantiquities

from the omission of "armored" from a military contract

to the omission of armor

from the omission of a phoneme from a language
to an obsolete language

from the obsolescence of our capacity to believe our own narrative
to the deconstruction of narrative

from the outsized euphony of elision
to the slur

despite the rain that falls obliquely
on peat smoldering years after fire

one only needs one truly beautiful story
one rusty index of moribund rhododendrons

on the underside of the sagging chain-link fence. One dandelion puffed out
in a standing ovation.

One origin.
One sacred place
       where phonemes do have use value
       where quarks and queues have use value
       where rasterization and rationing have use value
       where solar flares, a wireless signal from a deeper past
       where titanium spotlights and ultraviolet tanning beds
       where verified passwords preserved past expiry
       where a wealth of whitewash and wicker
       where xeric scrub devours a glockenspiel
       where our zodiac goes to rest, wakes

in one big bang
its patterns seared into space
like a polar sunburn under black lace

and the problem is, I can't see anything
past the two-way mirror of what's marketed to me

and the problem is, our language is a shell company
that needs rebranding

and the problem is, our debt, like our universe
keeps packing on the pounds

and it's getting to be a problem
all this perfectly extraordinary compulsory expanding   all this

       Plenty of parking
       Plenty of waterfront
       property allocated for the new amusement
       park and condominium complex
       provided we preserve the historical context
       Plenty of privacy
       Picnic tables, a gated
       promenade patrolled by city-funded private security
       A pharmacy and day care for residents
       with provisional acceptance, just your name to hold

your place. Here, anything is

possible. I promise

a profit before the end of the quarter

not just for the private sector but across every tax bracket

in the general populace. No, we can't accurately

predict how much and when. That forecast is

privileged. We don't need to ask for

permission. Every investment is

a potential win if you put the right spin on it. I say this

place is pure profit in the pocket.

They call me a prophet when in fact

I'm a poet, but even poetry is not a project

of this precise scale and orchestration. This is

a place to plump your pillow, lay your noggin. This is

a place where we polish your picket fence

A place where pets are pampered

A place where power exits the eye of the beholder

and props up everything it graces

from the proud custodian

to the pomp of the doorman, this is

a place of prosperity and improvement. Now

please remove your vehicle

from the premises.

Please

Preserve yourself

Please no one but yourself

Have patience, the grass will soon be ice cream
A new language will print itself into existence, so preserve
the present. Preserve your best loves, your last loves, your least loved

as though they are petrified forests and you are Plexiglass
as though they are phosphorus plumes and you are a pewter tanglewood
as though they are pale and underprepared for a voyage under the sun
for them, you must pretend
your pint-sized life isn't similarly moored with the same slipknots

you must permit your life to be equally moored with the same slipknots
you must live

        as quartz sparks when cracked

        as questions
        spark the crevasse

        you are an arrow in its quiver

        you are the quarry that feeds
        the queer chandelier

        you are the quarantine

        you preserve what
        quickens

(so go ahead—Question my motives;
ask me my name
Question my involvement
in the lighting of candles;
ask me why I left

my suitcase in the airport
when I boarded the plane
What kind of emergency
we could be avoiding
Question my pockets

my drill bits, my drill bits
Ask me if will I please
step in your office
your office, the office
if I am a homeowner

if I am a homemaker
if I am a homewrecker
if I am a man or a woman
a woman, a question
a question, a man

RIDERDUST (THE FAIRGROUNDS)

***

According to the
renowned phenomenologist,
the river is flat.

Its movement contains
no premodern figures of
continuous temporality.

Its movement contains spaces
which are not themselves
anthropological

and which do not
integrate earlier spaces.
Nor do they promote

earliness
to the status of
office. Its movement

contains,
and someday some delta
will have this much more sand.

vellum

vespers,
wrought-iron

cusps

***   *—if the river*
could give to you, could explain
to you in verse, could quote

could say—
a surface lives, it has been
born— then what

could I give
to give gifting
to you, my sound

I make with my hands—

as an aging expression gathers
a drawstring in a semi-smile:
This logo
     for you you
I would plot I would
to your plot, I would
ablate the spectrum of would. I would
rush, flash, whir, I would I would
a broken brown beer bottle would I
with the sound
        I make

with my office. The sound
the incorporated sound I make
with my wrist, unwound / scapula
skipping waves engorged by waves
lit red in the neon of the Safeway.

Do you think that crow knows
he's standing in someone's parking spot?
That a river knows a bridge when it
crosses one? That the two pieces of hymnal
music we found at the river's edge, one
folded & fled, one wadded as though
by a fist & covered with bitumen, do they
know we picked them from the pile of spent
Ernest & Julio Gallo, pitched them back in?
& have you ever pressed your tongue

against the river
in the middle of the night
in a monsoon?

I bet it tastes like
licorice

catfish nougat with olive meringue
pungent halvah potstickers braised
in mushroom kelp tartar, pike nectar
carob cellulose sumac baklava
laced with norwegian lime resin
salt omelet, tannic soufflé, foamflower
mimosa with barberry flour
vanilla pigeon confectionary
plum lorgnette in carrion gin
flambé, hickory-smoked lion's paw
with apple-cinnamon radish,
whitewashed trout in antler milk
braised in a blizzard of kiwi lint
raspberry sherry
horehound candy *again*
carrion gin *again*
again

again

No stone
makes of you

the sound you make when you laugh

                              (a wax bouquet with wire stem,
                                a moonscape organ unraveling
                                                                raveling
                        to velvet with the advantages of shades
                      to embellish homes of taste
with phantom maids

            so today I walked the river in remembrance.
            I walked to the place of the purple stones, sat   (
            on the bank and flicked purple stones into   unraveling
            the water. The water was the highest I've seen   raveling
            and the noises the stones made were dwarfed
            by its surging. The silt was busy with black   lazuline blades
            ants and casings of oak buds discarded, shells   laves, syncopated
            red and gummy stuck to my hands and left
            little red streaks like cuts, the smell of waxy
            cranberry Christmas candles and smeared dirt   chthonic
            in patches on my palms reminded me of the   caesura,
            petrichor of hay and eucalyptus in California,   accrued, accreted,
            my old navy suede coat with red stitching,
            the dandelions larger than Sacagawea dollars   bronzed, brazen, Byzantine

glinting, fast and yellow the joggers, dogs,
the unidentifiable insect I examined before
I left, its long pin body and folded window
wings resting right where I found the stone
with its center stained

                  like a geode, split

                           syrinx of sward & kine
                      diaphanous, oceanic eyelid
                              frothing ice-white
                           lattice
                            all
                    in the time it takes

                    a snowflake
             to melt on a wrist)   **where**

                         where

          stones dark
      as plums along the icy
        river's edge

     where
   in the typology
of national myth

                    where where

                      you must must

on the surface of water,
be calico. Cannot land,
cannot be forsythia, cannot

one yellow amongst reds,
not water, knows
of red water knows red

carbon. A crow, afraid

erodes. A fist of fir curls into
rust
a birch, pale as sandstone.

***

A birch, pale as sandstone,
erodes. A fist of fir curls into
rust
carbon. A crow, afraid

of red water knows red
not water, knows
one yellow amongst reds

cannot be forsythia, cannot
be calico, cannot land
on the surface of water.

***

What I meant to say was,

leaves

discarded two seasons ago,
gathered by crows.

What I meant to say

was,

black swans compose
themselves

where   the crows

are wearing

vintage clothes

where

where

I hear the water raging—
I hear the commuter rail—

its garland of thieves, its carpenter bees
tunnel through wooden spoons strung from trees
hawk-hooded like druids, hooked / hooks
to dreadnought / herringbone / store-bought / whore whore
amaranth, flagellant / stray's phosphorescent / teeth drainage age
foaming / feral Christmas wreaths / foxfire speak
in telephone canopies, the indelible / pure cane sugar
scream of F-117s—
/ roam

as contrails / concomitant
practice restraint

ragweed /
cut diamond / hologram / river

stutters / cuts

sultanic in the sun

·   *the little gods*

/ from us—

where pebbles pockmarked the slush I remember
where a sidewalk drunk with water I remember
had fallen into slumber. It was here I remember
that the path forked, one direction I remember
tapering into the paved and salted, I remember
where crooks of ebony trunks curved I remember
out of cracks in the asphalt, bare I remember
branches black and hooked as though I remember
the cracks themselves had sprouted I remember
and domed the deepening avenue I remember
Dead pines brushed their gray fingers remembering
against the elms' gnarled fists I remember
as the oaks snagged their neighbors' remembering
darkening vertebrae. Above the rolling I remember
marble of soot and snow, the natural mortal
world bristled in a skeletal glow glow
I stared up into the diffuse whiteness remembering
and saw that the clouds had grown sullen remembering
variegated in fluted shades like microcline remembering
feldspar where they jutted into the remembering
atmosphere, sunlight a lean trace of pyrite remembering
laced through the swollen opacity of the remembering
crystals— and at the base of the sky I remember
the rusted tatting of a Ferris wheel I remember

The river's crumpled
foil becomes less
a depth than a
surface below the
geometric eaves
of the Doubletree,
beneath the oak
that hangs over
the water like a
coat hook inverted,
the buds of its
skinny branches
about to burst like
match-heads into
green electricity

The river bows
like a thread of
ivy pressing
against glass,
pressing against
the iced arc of
shallow sand-
stone as if
magnetically
attracted to
the ledge of
the bend where
the smell of
sulfur hovers,
foaming

I remember
I remember
I remember
I remember
I remember
I remember
I remember
I remember
I remember
I remember
I remember
I remember
I remember
remember
foaming

foaming	foaming	foaming
foaming	foaming	foaming
foaming	foaming	foaming
foaming	foaming	foaming
foaming	foaming	foaming
foaming	foaming	foaming
foaming	foaming	foaming
foaming	foaming	foaming
foaming	foaming	foaming
foaming	foaming	foaming
foaming	foaming	foaming
foaming	foaming	foaming
foaming	foaming	foaming
foaming	foaming	remember
foaming	foaming	foaming

So remember

to pass to the quarterback.
It's the only way we'll
win. Remember. Time is
precious. The space
we occupy, from the road
to the rotary,
from the fight ring
to the ten yard line,
is precious.
    Remember,

when you stroke your paisley tie,
how the design
    reminds you
of parsley. How you know
the hostess
only resents you
because you can afford to eat.
    So remember

her name. Remember
her name. Remember

the bamboo raft
and the rope
that binds it. Remember

the monarch butterfly
and how
the chrysalis bled. Remember

your mother's redress/red dress.
        Remember
your friend
who changed her name to Venus.
        Remember

the fat tick
and the ankle that fed it.
        Remember
the pit bull
who refused to bite.
        Remember

every living thing
has a mouth.
        Remember
how hard it is to stand in line.
        Remember
how hard it is to stand

in the choir, unable
to sing.
        Remember
the salamander
in the mud beneath
the painted planter.

How we couldn't believe
he wasn't hungry
for light.
        Remember

how the rusty parking meters
aligned
        like red pinheads on a map
        like credits scrolling
        like a ribbon
        delimited only by its own frayed edge
        rising up the spinal ridge of the continent.
        Remember

the rolling blackouts
of retro fashions. Remember
the radioactive isotopes
in the rainwater's repetitions. Remember
he who fits the bridle holds the reins. Remember
how rapid eye movement

can be mistaken for dreams. Remember
the ripcords of high-volume
rapid assembly, the rattle, ring, roar. Remember
off-roading in the power lines. How the butterflies
rocked the weeds. How you prayed

the recall was effective. How attempting
to revoke an accident's ripple is like trying
to revise a rainbow. Remember

      should there be illness unattended until the onset of terminal coma—
      should there be love lost in the sweepstakes—

      should mockingbirds unlearn their infinities—
      should you slice yourself shaving, open a stain thaw-tender as calves in carlight—

      Save your childhood home from burning.
      Slum no more to be safe and void.

      A smokescreen, silver screen, sachet sewn with rose hip and sacrifice— somewhere
      someone (small font, passive voice) is stitching

      a silver heirloom into a hem
      she knows few survive

      the hatch marks of a telescopic lens— *smoke*
in the pines— where pines devour starlets. As the person before you

in the supermarket, the laundromat, the post office—*Stars,*
They're Just Like Us!— opines on the starlets.

So many times we've licked our postage.
So many times we've folded laundry.

We speak of ourselves as though it were our superpower

as somewhere, someone (small font, active voice)
sings the theme song to "Jeopardy." As someone

across the street mows the lawn in the drizzle. As you struggle
to speak of yourself gracefully. Living
in the suburbs, you are in danger

of slipping, of allowing
your self and your most interesting moments to be people and minutes you've left behind.
The times you stepped from the curb

to surrender yourself to the good and tragic.
In the suburbs, nothing
seems to happen. Nothing confessional lends

its story to the dirt. The hum of the dishwasher, the scent of thrift
store clothing, the continually looking outward into
a screen or a window and feeling

strange. When your neighbors post photos of themselves and their family, an endless
stream of streamers, cakes and babies, they, too, are
self-promoting. But they don't

see it that way. They think they are
sharing. All you have to share with the digital world is your
skull. Your circular

strolls through the state forest no longer induce
in you a sense of longing. You almost wish you could miss them. So instead of taking a walk
or sitting on your porch

and staring into the diffuse residue of northern wilderness, you
stand at your stereo as a soul record spins. Its sleeve
smells of cut grass and rain. There must be a word for the nostalgia you feel

for something that never happened. There must be a word for the foreboding you feel
when you think back on the past. There must be a word for the gaps in the music. The loud-
soft, stop and start. It sounds like no other silence, except, perhaps

the silence that follows the disappearance of wind chimes from a neighbor's tree.
A sound that makes it possible to live
the way a man in a cabin once lived, connected

to something in the earth beneath him. A man, a son of a man, who couldn't possibly
see missiles in the acorns, who couldn't possibly hear
sparrows use codewords when they speak, or interpret

the stalks of sumac in a vacant lot as protesters contesting its vacancy.

(My sister, my secretary,
my Sony,
my Steinway,

Because I love you I
save you
the best part of the animal

Because I love you I
save you
the best part of the vegetable

Because I love you I
cut you
the biggest slice of pie

the crisp
foot of the loaf because
you love
to chew and chew Because
you love

me I save you the magazines

because

you love to clip them and

so do I

CHAMPION MILL

VARIATIONS ON A FIELD, MISSOULA, MT

there is a buoyancy to ice unencoded
there is a buoyant blossom in spectacle
no part comes naturally part is work
and the days work and the aphids
the telomeres and tentative wrist
a glass quality in them now
a glass quality in the snow
a windshield embedded with spectacles
bedazzled quotients of ice
a windshield withstands elements
blue windshield supplants a sky
hazed red with rumor smoky
clavicles of turbines
cavities design

hooks in the shoulder of a byway
old rumor unproved appendix
a buoyancy in the shifting gear
gearshift of manual transmission
in tape loop lupine cellophane
rumor backpedals down the highway
but what of drift of hint in shag and
what of green flies and what of redux
platinum sparkplugs and what of harts
of speculative fiction spooks coils kisses
and what of domain walls and monopoles
and what of the trowel used to contuse
this water to describe dance
as curve of pursuit

a surface of a sphere is an approximation

a wily chaotic hoop of flagpole

a chimney stovepipe gyroscope caduceus

a shipboard compass computer

simulation a rotating plate of dust

and what of tibia of china and what lust

and what of siamese we

all a bit live a bit must

the brass quality of the gimbal

the brass quality of dusk

and what of radar

analogous to duel

of turbulence

of rust

somewhere a landfill with its callus

of cold beryllium

measured wind with foil fan

rebar skewed to violet

somewhere a window painted pink

closed its ear

archaic torso of a mill

decorated like a war veteran

its red and yellow tags

black tape lip

mouth ajar lets

weather in

what would a geologist do

with a heart like this

blue is symptom of a deeper malady

two kinds of blue   mesozoic pleiocene

neither intuitive neither dream

neither metacentric boundaries key

the violet blacklit landscape painting

its *nova totius terrarum orbis geographica*

its glittery theater of snowglobe

their fasciate obligate cartomancy

their theater of key with velvet rope

theater of scree of bruise of

wild unknowing wild

blackberry made bronze

by scarcity made barb wire

unable to uncrow

in deconstructing a minor key
in a popular book on an ancient world
from the hoover dam to cape canaveral
where do these stairs actually go
and why do black holes radiate energy
and why does this energy imply heat
and heat imply body and body
imply loss and why does slow loss
of heat suggest we evaporate slowly
and who does the black hole really love
and where does this aqueduct flow
and where do we store the silent
films no one screens anymore
and the end music why is it silver

go to field a periphery
go to a field with a friend
pass caricature paintings
past weed acrylic flint
and lay on your back arms spread
and lay in the black stink of park
earth convex against your harp
dirt flexed under mars
go without javelin corn or lens
and go without trial goal or fence
without the batsman will insist
without the batter will insist
and will assist
and will assist

what percent tungsten

                        percent lead

what lock shale of yellowcake

thread beams too damp to burn

pitch like a tent

somewhere a lack of firewood

strikes a blue match

somewhere a satellite seals

its mind cell by cell retires

its blueshift

sinks

in a drift

o what longing for drift

if there were no drift

Do you turn on your television for company?

Do you ever feel the urge to take a photograph?

Take waning at apogee— can you see the moon's nail scrape the sky?

The arrival of its thumb on the pole, its halo on the wire?

The bottleneck of a traffic jam rattles its tarnished brand.

Its echo is a drainage pipe spitting into brambles.

Its emergency trundle of sandbags and klieg lights.

Its razorblade address. Its supermoon magnet.

Its tail end is spectrum, tapering to pallor

in rhinestones on the asphalt sky,

in the glint of a dun lure in black water,

a helicopter

where an unlikely joy overwhelms me. Says come see me,
keys my name into a sapling. Says once we
learn to step over the broken platter, we'll never be the same.
Mimosa blossoms bob on the tasteless river. We will

never paint over them. The orange leaves. The trees' pallbearers.
The body aches after fixing cars all day. The blisters on our fingers
after cutting hearts from paper. The cigarette, the fog so thick
you can't tell there's smoke. Black dogs, black coffee, black licorice.

The graphite town. The refillable pencil town. Tracings of property lines.
The hot air balloon. Carrying color. By fire.
The merry-go-round, the children laughing— about what— they'll forget.
The missed exits and U-turns. Upended stone walls.

The man who cuts hair, desperate for just a few chips to bargain.
The woman who swabs the checkerboard floor.
The youth rips a razor from his pigskin wallet.
There are shipwrecks no one explores.

And there is reason, blank bankbooks, saddle-stitched specifics.
Where a red clay storm is stirring up the allergens.
The rusted clover has taken on the odor of an oath.
You must think of yourself as ammunition.

To keep present the body, in theory, in flames.
To remember that part of what you breathe is volatile.

Theory flies from you like red yarn from the hull of a diesel flail.
The thresher afire, fire chewing chaff like boll weevils suckling kudzu.

Unearth the begonias wrap their roots in plastic.
Unearth the hydrangea pack it in bubble wrap.
Unearth the pachysandra, ochre kindling.
It's not an unreasonable use of force.

If you verify your identity
If vines of fluid trickle through your fractured windshield

Violins forgive bows. Do bows forgive?
Visit historical monuments, narrate the exquisite chronicle of the arsenic-fed

Voluminous vessels hazardous with hydrogen
The wasps' locket smacked down, their frail kettle-jewels lacquered with luminous poisons

Wasps build because they love the building
We inherited our fear of strangers in stairwells

We're tired of the clutter
We tenderly commit this body to the ground

What would you do if you came upon you in this corridor of cut grass?
What wound would you bias in the triage?

When two bells ring close enough together in time, one sound is heard, but
Where does the sky end and the reed begin?

Whether farewells
Whether war, in context, is just

White mid-afternoon moon behind streaks of cirrus

Will your child be using a car seat during flight?

                    Why?

Wool shrinks like industry
Wire spirals in uniform silos

Would I sell you Xanax, wilted petunias?
Would I tell you we injected blue dye into the river?
    We can

            You know

                    What they say on Thanksgiving.
                            They say: *what a beautiful bird.*

Your anorexic patron
Your anonymous file transfer protocol

> Your broken bamboo, your thyme tincture
> Your hound anesthetized to restrain her from spinning

Your locus of influence on the billions served, your UPS deliveryman, a feather
As you clean your tongue with your knife

> Your silver Zippo, your zip code, a yellowjacket in your Coke can
> Your view blurred by the motorcade

> Your *who remembers who forgets*
> Your xylophone is missing

> Your yellow ribbon
> Your zinfandel fouled by black cork rot

> Zinnias ablaze—
> Zirconium rods ablaze—

(Adze, because the sky
is chocolate

Adze, because the clouds
ablaze

Adze, because the diner
is lit
like an embassy

Adze, because the counter
is proof
we are penetrable

Adze, because hunger
orders
the largest plate

Adze, because the waitress
loads cakes
into the revolver

Adze, because the cherry blossoms
aren't real
Because what isn't real
is permanent

AMERICAN FLAGS

In the 20th century, the artists split
into camps. Anger and violence and weird sex
shaped every corner of theory.

The fiber artists stole thread.
The performance artists were arrested
at the bank, each with one hand on the butt

of a gun, one hand on the glass. Now, we offer
a toast to old art, a toast to the zoo,
because we know the mystery

of memory is not concealed
in the higher animal (it is concealed
in the route) and because the elephant

isn't Thailand's only
low-emission form of transport.
We will always have imagination.

We will always have a beautiful day
after tomorrow.

+

Day is near. It is a question now.

Even a bird can see the moonlight is a sham.

Slowly, slowly the gears. The dark, the dark encapsulates.

The moon is near carboxylate now.

The circles are filled. Into the machine, my choices.

One-syllable wisps of air.

One-syllable wisps of air.

Is it possible to sum up the Arab Spring
using only the physical characteristics

of women? (Anonymous, I turn
the background yellow

as though the page is a bright kitchen
where health and healing

come conjoined.)
(I fall asleep

looking at others, looking
for others, searching

for others.) (Aren't we all?
Isn't heaven?)

+

We never thought of growing old together.
We thought of being each other.
We realized we were Great Danes
with heads of 19th-century cameras.
We were sharpshooters beginning or ending
anything with one shot. We shot
to paralyze. Then made them feel.

.

SAW MILL PARKWAY, YONKERS, NY

I drive 75 miles
to and from
work, thinking.

Either a woman is someone
or she is not. Either a war

is a war
or it is not.

+

Your key is the shiniest thing in the storm drain.
My key is the tiniest paralysis.
Your key is in a tunnel with a book of matches.
My key is trying to play the drums.
Your key fills the boxes and mails them Priority.
My key needs space
more than it needs boxes.

In my nightdream, now
my daydream, a widowed man
fastens his eyes on a pretty young girl.

I feel like I've known you for years, he tells her.
He doesn't know she'll steal his credit cards
and merge two people into one

identity like a pair of answers
to a single question.

I don't have to look young, he says.
I don't have to look happy.
Old customs of mourning no longer apply.

He exits left on the highway
to expressions of innocence and eloquence and rhyme.
It has to be personal somehow, he says.

It must be part of your personal fabric.
It's good to be at home with yourself,
especially when driving.

No one is more defenseless than when
they are driving alone under the sky.

+

Lost cat. Grey with some tan flecks.
A wasteland companion.
You never actually own him.
You merely take care of him.
I wanted to be him.
The oddball classicist.
The vein in your work.

LINCOLN TUNNEL, NEW YORK, NY

Like a car, the mind runs
poorly.

My tunnel's exit is now
the entrance. I'm not

sure when I first felt
time slipping

in and out
of the innards of clocks.

Time is bizarre.
Traffic and food and love are bizarre.

The tunnels we build
are bizarre.

Just look

at the yellow sodium light
of our city's permanent imagination.

+

A building is an exterior
that narrates the interior.
Tell me this in a language
that I can understand. Tell me
the other side is grass. Tell me
the sun is inside us. Help me
frame this photograph.

The Dead C Scrolls

J is apocrypha.

J is black keys.

J is the cannon bone.

J is Cease and Desist.

J is her coat pockets full of rocks.

J declines comment.

J declines your tag request.

J don't you dare repeat that in front of your father.

J is the feminine voice.

J flip-flops.

J flows from the Aral Sea to the North Pacific Gyre.

J is G♭, A♭, B♭, D♭, E♭,

then J is C#, D#, F#, G#, A#.

J is HIV-positive.

J stuck her head in the oven to light the pilot light.

J is incoming calls only.

J is last call.

J is macular degeneration.

J is moon void of course.

J is the one whose name cannot be spoken because no one exists before J to name J.

J is an orange rectangular prism approximately 13" × 7" × 5"

J is pitchy.

J is the scar where a pit bull bit your leg. It was your fault. You pulled its tail.

J is not tall enough to ride this ride.

J surrendered in the Marxist analysis.

J is "This sentence is false."

J is undefined.

J was voted off the island.

J is where I'm calling from.

J will speak for itself.

Notes

The Greenpoint Terminal Market complex occupied over three blocks of land along the East River between Greenpoint Avenue and Oak Street in Greenpoint, Brooklyn. Built by the American Manufacturing Company, once the largest manufacturer of rope and jute in the world, the 16-building warehouse complex was later used as a storage facility for recycled polyester material and clothing. The Municipal Art Society of New York, the Metropolitan Waterfront Alliance, and the Preservation League of New York State were struggling to preserve the structure as a historic landmark when the complex burned to the ground in 2006.

As Moscow's inland location provided no suitable venue at which to stage the sailing event for the 22nd Summer Olympic Games in 1980, the USSR's Olympic organizing committee looked to seaside Tallinn, the capital of the Estonian Soviet Socialist Republic. The V. I. Lenin Palace of Culture and Sport was completed in Tallinn in time for the games, and included a concert hall, a heliport, and an outdoor park. The complex was later renamed *Linnahall* after Estonia regained its independence in 1990. Although the concrete building has decayed significantly, it is occasionally used for concert events. In early 2010, Tallinn Entertainment, founded by Ronald S. Lauder, CEO of cosmetics giant Estée Lauder, signed a 99-year lease with the local government to develop the structure into a casino.

The Champion Mill was a lumber mill located on the south bank of the Clark Fork River in Missoula, Montana. Just west of Ogren Field, home of Missoula's minor league baseball team, the decommissioned mill site was regarded as a symbol of the lost glory days of Montana's logging industry. The building was demolished and its surrounding area decontaminated and rezoned for mixed-use in 2008.

From "V. I. Lenin Palace of Culture and Sport" and "Riderdust (The Fairgrounds)": Discussing his departure from representation in his 1915 painting *Black Square*, Acmeist and Russian Suprematist painter Kazimir Malevich said: "But a surface lives, it has been born."

Acknowledgments

Many thanks to the editors and staff of *American Letters & Commentary*, *Aufgabe*, *Blackbird*, *Housefire*, *New South*, *The Seattle Review*, *Stolen Island*, and *Verse* for sharing these poems and for allowing their reprint with grateful acknowledgment.

Selections from this manuscript appear in *Listening for Earthquakes*, first runner-up in the 2011 Caketrain Chapbook Contest, selected by Rosmarie Waldrop, and *Rewilding*, winner of the 2012 Ahsahta Press Chapbook Contest, selected by Cathy Park Hong.

"Champion Mill" appears in *The Arcadia Project: North American Postmodern Pastoral*, an anthology edited by Joshua Corey & G.C. Waldrep (Ahsahta Press).

Many thanks to the Connecticut Office of the Arts and to the Foundation for Contemporary Arts for the time and financial support.

JASMINE DREAME WAGNER is the author of *Rewilding* (Ahsahta Press, 2013) and *Listening for Earthquakes* (Caketrain Journal and Press, 2012). Her writing has appeared in *American Letters & Commentary*, *Blackbird*, *Colorado Review*, *Indiana Review*, *NANO Fiction*, *New American Writing*, *Seattle Review*, *Verse*, and in two anthologies: *The Arcadia Project: North American Postmodern Pastoral* (Ahsahta Press, 2012) and *Lost and Found: Stories from New York* (Mr. Beller's Neighborhood Books, 2009). A graduate of Columbia University and the University of Montana, Jasmine has received grants and fellowships from the Connecticut Office of the Arts, Foundation for Contemporary Arts, Hall Farm Center for Arts & Education, Summer Literary Seminars–Kenya, and The Wassaic Project. She teaches creative writing at Western Connecticut State University.